In memory of Betty Irene Patch
17/02/29 – 7/11/17

Keep on giggling Patchy!

Aunt Bet's Ramblings & Giggles

Who was Aunt Bet?

Imagine a jolly, loving and generous little old lady, add a sprinkling of raw wit and a glint in the eye and you've got 'Patchy'.
Not an aunt in the family sense, but a god-mother to my mother, so an aunty she was. Loved by all and partial, or should I say VERY partial to the odd glass of sherry!
Born in central Somerset before the war where she remained. She never married and worked all her days in the local butcher.
A religious girl at heart and the church was a big focus in her life.

Why create this book?

My mother found one of her old notebooks of jokes jotted down some time between 1929 and 2017.
Rather than let them stay hidden, I thought I would put them in a book.
Who knows how many Christmas crackers she pulled or jokes she exchanged at the Women's Institute, but these jokes came from somewhere.
She found them funny enough to write down and keep, so I hope you do as well.

For my mum.

A few of my mum's memories...

We went to the seaside and parked in the car park as you do.
As we were leaving the car park a police officer appeared and our Betty said to him.
'There is somebody here you can lock up' she joked pointing and clearly meaning me.
He said 'No thank you we have enough of that sort already.'

How embarrassing...

Another time we went to Exmouth in Devon for the day. Whilst walking along the seafront there was large set of scales that you could put money in to weigh yourself.
We all took it in turns. Betty's turn arrived and she got on and the hand went all the way round the face of the machine, so she had broken it!

Ironically, she was a tiny lady.

The same day and a little further along the promenade there was a row
of deck chairs.

We all decided to sit on them and Barrie, my brother, went straight
through the bottom and got stuck.
He was a very big lad. Even at a young age 6ft+ tall.
My parents did laugh and so did I.

He didn't see the funny side and it was a real struggle to prise him free!

Wherever and whenever we went somewhere with Betty, we always
seemed to have some sort of mishap.

However, she always had a good giggle and always saw the funny side.

She did make it fun!

Here follows a rambling ...

If after church you wait a while.
Someone may greet you with a smile.
But, if you quickly rise and flee.
We'll all seem stiff and cold maybe.
The one beside you in the pew.
Is perhaps a stranger too.
All here, like you, have fears and cares.
All of us need each others kind prayers
In fellowship we bid you meet.
With us around god's mercy seat.

Now for her giggles!

Why did the Banana go out with a prune?

Because he couldn't find a date.

Teacher :
If you had 50 pence in one pocket and 75 pence in the other how much money would you have?

Pupil:
Someone else's trousers Miss!

A cat-burglar entered a house in the dark of night.

'Jesus is watching you... Jesus is watching you...'

Panicked, he looked around for the source of the whisper, when he finds a parrot in a cage, with the name "Eric" on it. Relieved, he says:

'Who named a parrot Eric?'

The parrot answers:

'The same person that named the guard dog Jesus'.

Seen on a church notice board.

Come early and get a back seat.

My electric blanket caught fire causing considerable damage and the insurance agent called to help complete the claim form.
Working through the questions he asked. 'Was the bed on fire when you got into it?'

I told my doctor that I broke my arm in
three places.

He replied,
'You should stop going to those places.'

A little boy pestered his reluctant
father into taking him to the zoo.
'So how was it?' asked his mother on
their return.
'It was great!' replied the little boy.
'AND daddy really liked it too, especially
when one animal came racing home at
thirty to one!'

Why did the scarecrow
win an award?

Because he was
outstanding in his field!

Old woman said with a wink:
'Come upstairs and give me a cuddle.'

Old man said with a sigh:
'I'm sorry, I don't think I can do both!'

How does a penguin build its house?

Igloos it together.

Why did the bicycle fall over?

It was two-tired.

Did you hear about the guy who invented Lifesavers?

He made a mint!

I told my mother she should embrace her mistakes.

She gave me a hug.

A Bishop was astonished to hear a little girl say that you had to be brave to go to church.

'Why do you say that?' He asked.

'Well, I heard my uncle tell my aunt last Sunday that there was a canon in the pulpit, that the choir murdered the anthem, and that the organist had then drowned the choir!'

You know you're getting older when you have a party and the neighbors don't realize it.

My doctor told me I need to start exercising.

So, every morning I do diddly-squats.

My memory's gotten so bad,
I started a "Remember List"... but I can't
remember where I put it.

When you're a young and spritely 20 year old and you drop something, you pick it up.
When you're 70 years of age and you drop something, you decide you don't need it anymore.

I'm not saying I'm old, but my back goes
out more than I do.

I'm reading a book on anti-gravity.

It's impossible to put down!

The older I get, the earlier it gets late.

I don't need anger management;

I need people to stop making me mad!

I asked my grandkids what a meme is.
They said it's something that went viral.

I thought,

'Like the flu?'

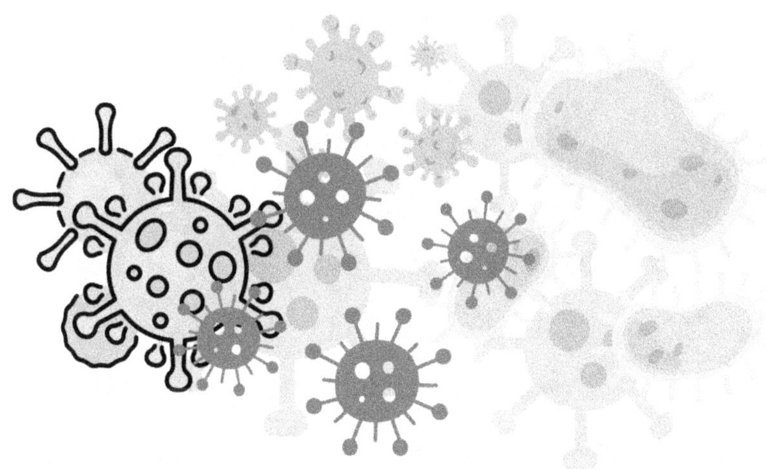

Patient: 'Doctor, you have to help me, I think I can see in the future.'

Doctor: 'When did it start?"

Patient: 'Next week.'

I asked my wife if I was getting old and
out of shape.

She said, 'You've always been out of shape,
but at least you're consistent.'

Doris Carter shared another of her amusing stories about her Pastor grandfather's congregation . It concerned the general plumber. He had not been in the habit of attending church regularly.

When he retired he started coming more often.

Doris's grandfather told him that it was nice to see him so regularly now that he had retired.

The old plumber explained 'It's not the service Pastor, it's just the wife likes me out of the house whilst she cooks Sunday lunch'

'I've been having trouble with rheumatism today, Mr Jones.'
said young Billy.
'I say you're rather young to have rheumatism!' replied Mr Jones the teacher.
'Oh no it's not that Mr Jones. I'm just having great difficulty spelling it!'

I couldn't help, but chuckle at the story
I heard about the teenage lads who
were standing on the corner opposite
the church one Sunday evening in
December.
One was heard to say.

'I don't know who this Carol Service is,
but she certainly packs them in!'

Old age makes us great multitaskers.

Why, I can sneeze and pee at the same time!

What goes up but never comes down?

Your age.

What's worse than middle age?

Knowing you'll grow out of it.

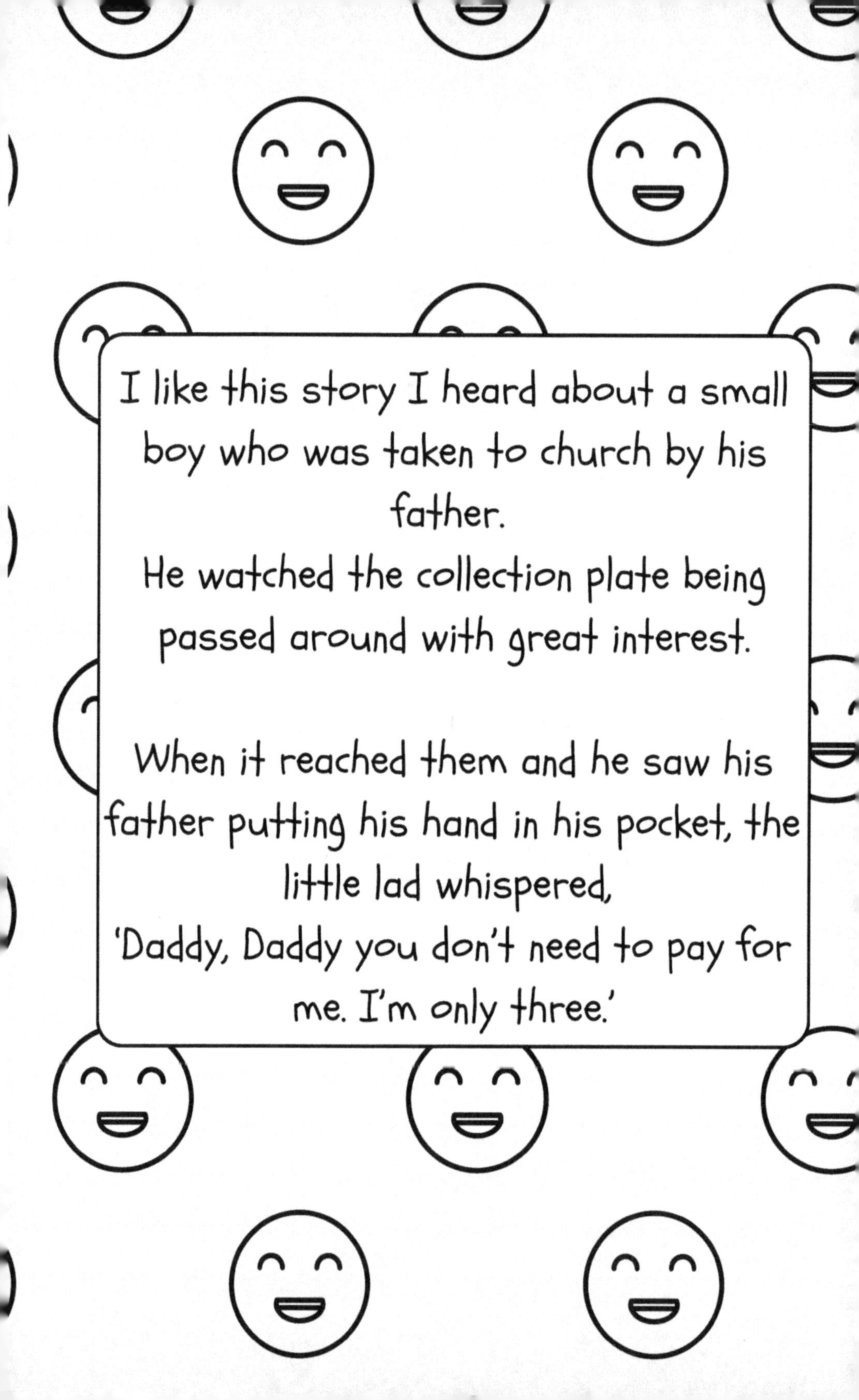

I like this story I heard about a small boy who was taken to church by his father.

He watched the collection plate being passed around with great interest.

When it reached them and he saw his father putting his hand in his pocket, the little lad whispered,

'Daddy, Daddy you don't need to pay for me. I'm only three.'

What did one plate say to the other?

'Lunch is on me!'

At my age, the only pole dancing I do is while holding on to the safety bar in the bathtub.

A father was reading Bible stories to his young son. He read, 'The man named Lot was warned to take his wife and flee out of the city, but his wife looked back and was turned into a pillar of salt.'

His son asked,
'What happened to the flea?'

Why don't oysters share their pearls?

Because they're shellfish!

How does a cucumber
become a pickle?

It goes through a
jarring experience.

Aunty Ivy tripped and took a heavy fall at
the coffee shop.

Fortunately, she didn't break anything, not
even a single plate or saucer.

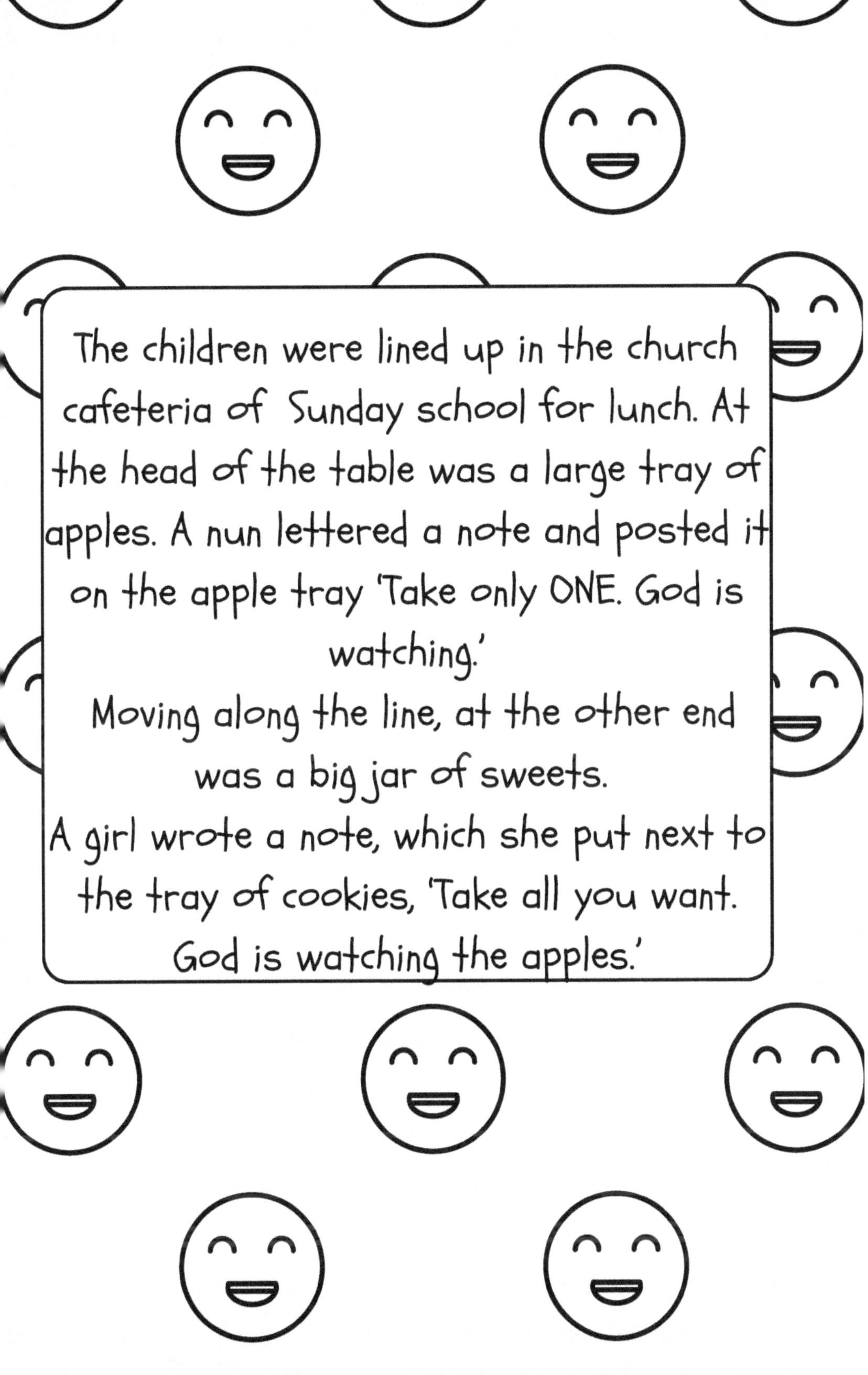

The children were lined up in the church cafeteria of Sunday school for lunch. At the head of the table was a large tray of apples. A nun lettered a note and posted it on the apple tray 'Take only ONE. God is watching.'

Moving along the line, at the other end was a big jar of sweets.

A girl wrote a note, which she put next to the tray of cookies, 'Take all you want. God is watching the apples.'

My toddler and I were shopping when a
heavily tattooed man walked by.

My daughter's eyes grew wide as she said.
'I'll bet his mummy took all his felt tips
away!'

My sister rang her husband to be on
the way home from work and asked
him to peel the potatoes.
When she arrived she noticed that he
had only managed one spud.
He said that he couldn't get to grips
with the new fangled, expensive potato
peeler.

Then she saw he had been trying to do
the job with a tin opener.

A Sunday school teacher asked her little children as they were on their way to the church service.

'And why is it necessary to be quiet in church?'

One bright little lass piped up. 'Because people are sleeping Miss.'

For our pastor's 70th birthday, the congregation decided to give him a new suit.

He was so touched by the gift that the following Sunday he stood before everyone and, with tears in his eyes, announced, "Today I am preaching to you in my birthday suit."

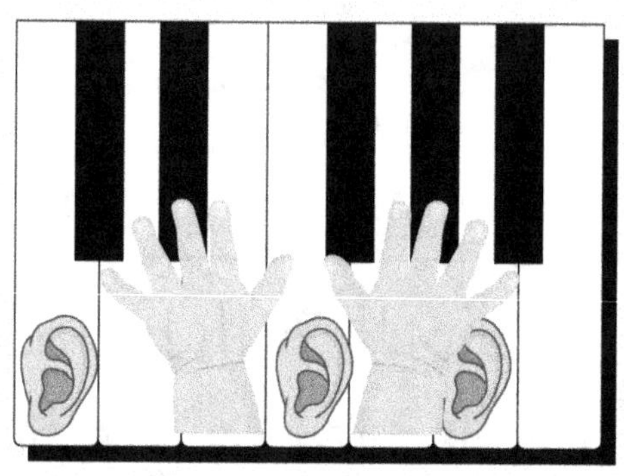

'Do you play the piano?'
'Yes, I play by ear!'

'Oh! I thought you played it with your
hands!'

A double glazing salesman phoned one of his customers.

'Hello, Mr Brown.' he said.
'I'm calling because we fitted your new windows a year ago and you haven't made any payments yet.'

To which the man replied.
'But you said that these windows would pay for themselves in 12 months!'

During World War II a French cheese factory was destroyed.

Debris was everywhere.

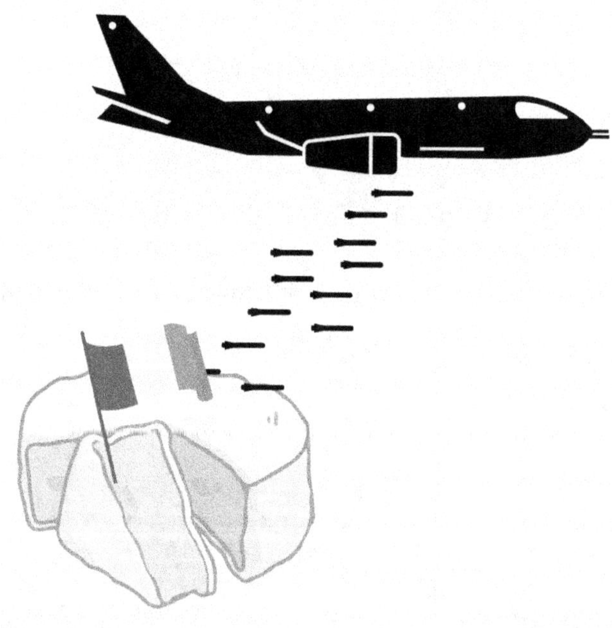

After I'd had a nasty fall on a broken paving stone in our road, my young grand daughter aged six said to me.
'Nanna, you should go and see the man from the council and tell him you want constipation money!'

My five year old son Jack was pretending to play rock drums by hitting the furniture with sticks.

He then began to play more slowly and his dad asked. 'What are you doing, now?'

'Playing classical music!' he replied.

A married couple were asleep when the
phone rang at 2am. The wife picked up the
phone, listened and said.
'How should I know that's a 100 miles
from here?'and hung up.
The husband asked 'Who was that?'
The wife replied 'I don't know.
Some women wanted to know if the coast
was clear!'

I went to the butcher's the other day and I bet £50 that he couldn't reach the meat off the top shelf.

He didn't take the bet in the end as the steaks were too high.

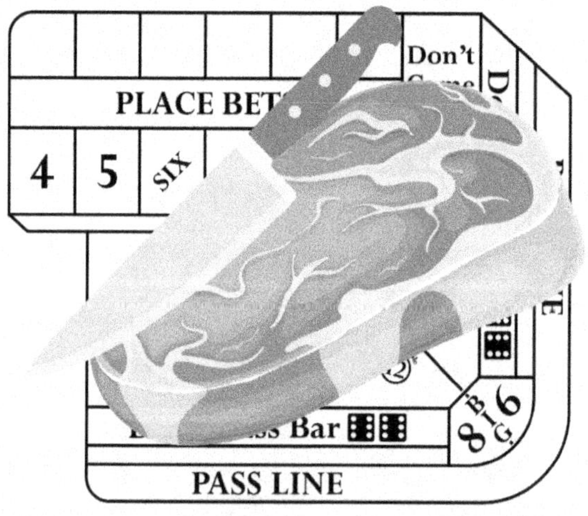

My grandparents fought during World War
II.

They ended up getting a divorce.

I was giving my grandson, Tom SPECIAL
sweets because the poor lamb had the
measles, BUT Paula his three year old
sister asked if she could have the measles
when he finished with them...

I couldn't help, but give her a treat too.

I was returning home on the bus from a wonderful day at the seaside with my daughter and two young grandsons.
Suddenly, one of the boys shouted in a deafening voice.
'Mum, didnt we have a fun day today burying grandma.'
He meant in the sand of course, but we certainly got some funny looks from the other passengers.

What do you call a shirt you go to war with?

A tank top!

When my two nephews, Jay five, and
Damon seven, were staying over with me I
asked them if they'd brushed their teeth
and spent a penny.

Jay answered 'Yes, I've cleaned my teeth,
but I haven't got any money to spend!'

It made me smile.

My friend's four year old
son Alastair was
admiring my new hair
colour and asked me
how it happened.
When I explained that it
had come out of a
bottle he replied.
'Oh, how much did you
have to drink then?'

What do you say when a grandpa, his son, and his grandson all hear a joke, laugh a lot, and wet their pants?

It runs in their 'jeans'.

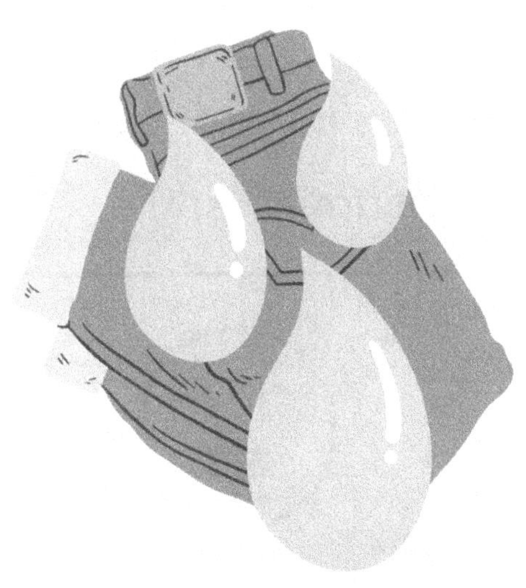

We took our grand daughter, Rebecca five, to a christening and told her there would be a party afterwards, she was so excited.
In the church when the lady brought the collection plate around she said to her.

'I'll have chicken nuggets, please' with a beaming smile.

I was in the supermarket
with my three year old son
the other day when he called
from the toy section.

'Daddy you need to get some
marbles!'

'We got lots at home I told
him'

'But mummy said you've lost
yours!'

He shouted so everyone could
hear.

My friend Doris and I went to the seniors yoga session today.

It was easy for me, but it was quite of a stretch to her.

My friend is always getting her words
mixed up.
The other day she was telling me about
her niece who was trying for a baby.
'She's had her first fertilizer treatment'
she told me.

I couldn't help, but imagine her niece
standing beside a bag of soil!

During a school RE lesson a discussion about creation broke out.

Teacher: Who do you think was the fastest person in the bible?

Student: Adam! Because he came first in the human race.

'Dad, are you growing taller all the time?'
asked the curious son.

'No, son I'm sure I have stopped now.
Why do you ask?'

'Cause the top of your head is poking up
through your hair.'

What do you call a parade of rabbits
hopping backwards?

A receding hare-line.

I used to be addicted to the Hokey-
Cokey, (Hokey-Pokey)
but then I turned myself around.

That's what its all about apparently...

How do you make holy water?

You boil the hell out of it.

Why did the king go to the dentist?

He needed a crown.

How did Noah sail his Ark at night?

Using floodlights.

Why did the frog take the bus to work?

His car got toad.

My five year old grandson visited while
I was watching an episode of a soap
on television where a baby was being
born.

Braced for questions I had to laugh
when he chipped in saying.
'I don't know why he's making so much
fuss I didn't when I was in hospital!'

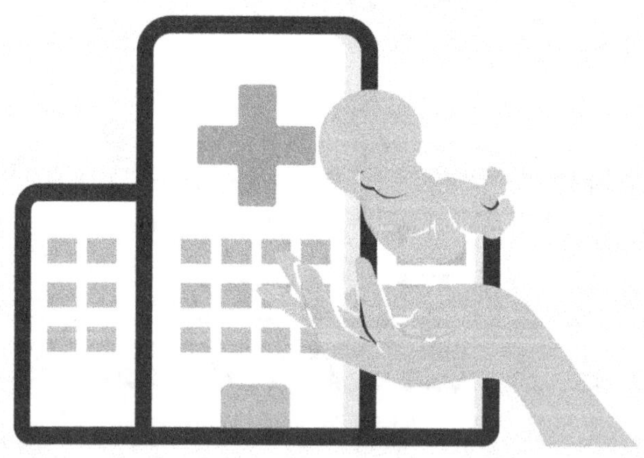

How long did Cain hate his
brother?

As long as he was able! (Abel)

Doctor: Nurse, how is that little girl doing who swallowed two shillings and six pence last night?

Nurse: No change yet.

I went with my daughter to her medical
clinic and helped fill out a form.
After Name and Address, the next question
was "Nearest Relative."
She wrote 'stood next to me.'

I was waiting for my prescription at
the chemist when a young woman
came and asked for a pregnancy test.

The assistant told her they stocked
three types and asked the woman
which of them she would like.
The woman smiled and said 'The one
that says I'm not!'

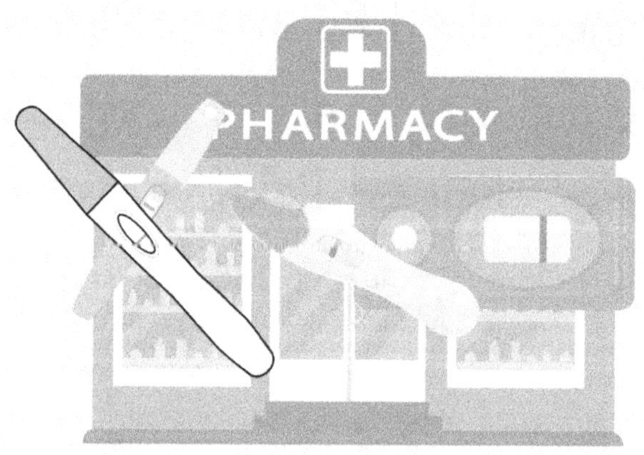

My great grandson, Amon aged nine, came
to visit me and went to the local park so
he could have a ride on his bike.
As I walked alongside while he wobbled a
little unsteadily he asked me.
'Nanna, can you ride a bike?'
I told him that I could ride a bike and he
said.
'I bet you can probably ride a bike
without stabilizers Nan!'

I took my grand daughter for a day
in the countryside and we noticed
some beautiful wild flowers growing
in the fields. In the corner of the field
there was a large bull.
'Can we pick some of those flowers?'
asked my grand daughter.
'We'd better not' I said' The bull
might charge'
'Don't worry nanna I've got some
money!' was her reply.

Did you hear about the octopus that held
up a convenience store?

It was an armed-robbery.

Every week I phone an elderly friend to see how she is doing. When I rang recently she complained that the road workers were outside her house all day long, and that they had given her an awful headache with the neurotic drill that they were using.

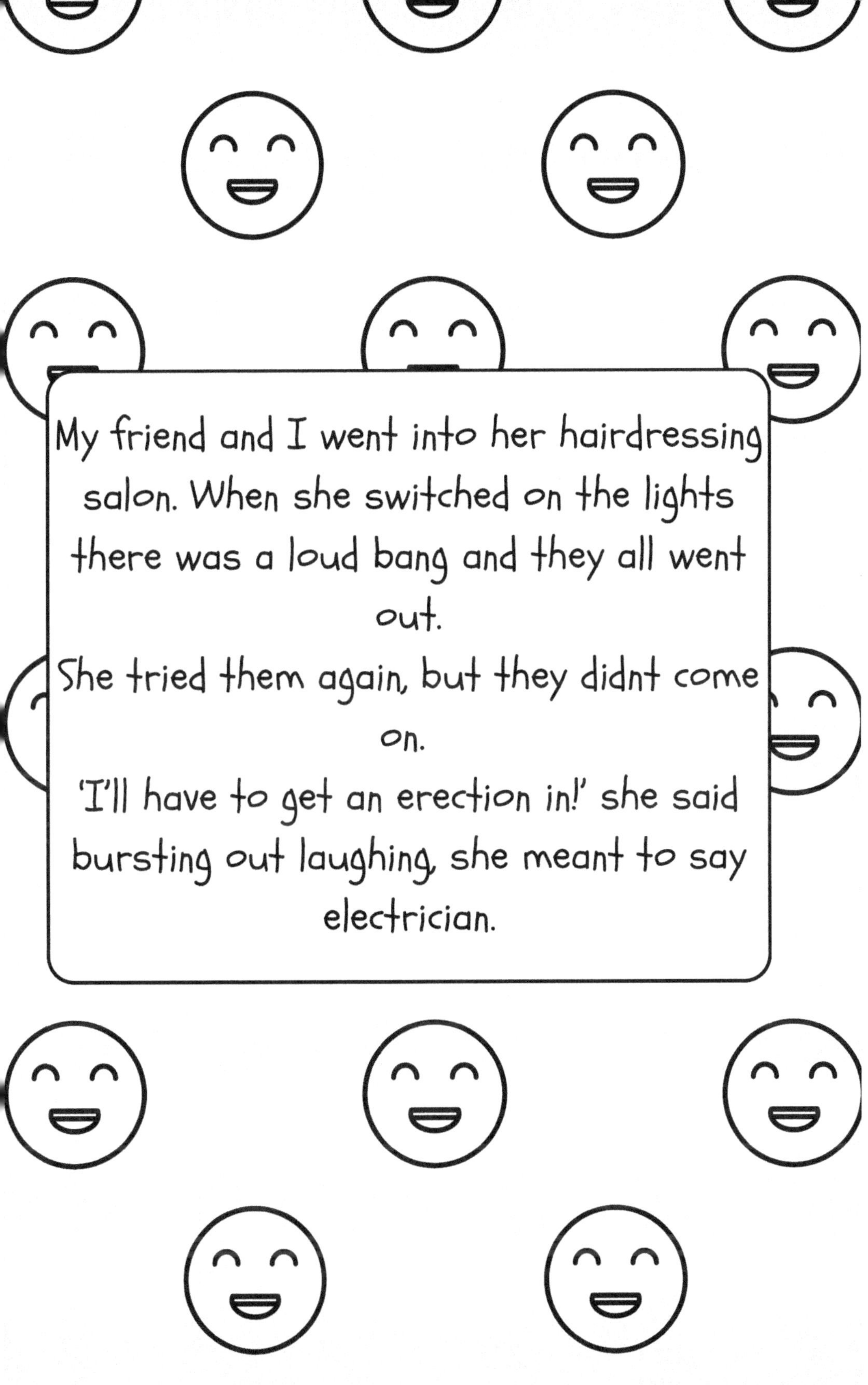

My friend and I went into her hairdressing salon. When she switched on the lights there was a loud bang and they all went out.
She tried them again, but they didnt come on.
'I'll have to get an erection in!' she said bursting out laughing, she meant to say electrician.

What falls in winter but never gets hurt?

Snow.

My grandson was being christened so we
took his little sister Michelle, aged four,
to the church.
She was fascinated by the vicar when he
poured the holy water over the baby's
head.
She said for all to hear.
'His heads not dirty, my mummy washed
the baby in the bath this morning.'

I phoned the local builder today and asked
him.
'Can I have a skip outside my house?'
He said.
'Sure. Go ahead. It's great exercise!'

Why did the teddy bear say no to dessert?

Because he was stuffed.

I'm wasn't a fan of facial hair,

but eventually it grew on me.

Why shouldn't pigs drive?

They hog the road.

Which king loved to do fractions?

Henry the 8th.

Sometimes I have a little chuckle to myself at the unintended humour from non-native English speakers.

Jenny had recently got her perfect job and was welcomed into the company by the CEO, who although foreign had lived in the UK for some years.

'It's good to have you here Jenny as you know we are a little underhanded.'

One teddy bear asked another teddy bear
where he lived.
'I'm not going to tell you that! You'll
steal all my clothes!'
As if teddies have clothes...

Why is six afraid of seven?

Because seven eight nine.

RIP, boiling water.

You will be mist.

What's the difference between a poorly dressed man on a tricycle and a well-dressed man on a bicycle?

Attire.

What do you call a fish without an eye?

Fsh.

Some Miner teddy bears had a day off and wanted to go to the woods to relax. Their foreman told them to be careful as TODAY could be the day the teddies get their picks-nicked.

What do you call a vicar on a moped?

Rev!

During a maths lesson a teacher tried to teach simple addition.
Teacher: 'If I had 8 bananas in one hand and 10 potatoes in the other hand, what would I have?'
Student: 'Big hands Sir!'

www.ingramcontent.com/pod-product-compliance
Lightning Source LLC
Chambersburg PA
CBHW050547160726
48003CB00002B/786